"I like all simple things, boiled eggs, oysters
and caviare, *truite au bleu*, grilled salmon,
roast lamb (the saddle by preference),
cold grouse, treacle tart and rice pudding.
But of all simple things the only one I can eat
day in and day out, not only without disgust
but with the eagerness of an appetite
unimpaired by excess, is macaroni."

From a short story, *The Hairless Mexican*
by W. Somerset Maugham

ANNA DEL CONTE'S

Italian Kitchen
LA PASTASCIUTTA

PASTA DISHES

ILLUSTRATED BY FLO BAYLEY

SIMON &
SCHUSTER

SIMON & SCHUSTER

SIMON & SCHUSTER
Simon & Schuster Building
Rockefeller Center
1230 Avenue of the Americas
New York, New York 10020

Designed by Andrew Barron & Collis Clements Associates
Typesetting by Selwood Systems, Midsomer Norton, Avon
Printed and bound in Italy by New Interlitho

10 9 8 7 6 5 4 3 2 1

Library of Congress Cataloging in Publication Data:
Del Conte, Anna.
  La pastasciutta : pasta dishes / by Anna del Conte.
    p.   cm. — (Anna del Conte's Italian kitchen)
  Includes bibliographical references and index.
  ISBN 0–671–87031–9 : $14.00
  1. Cookery (Pasta).   2. Cookery, Italian.   I. Title.
II. Series: Del Conte, Anna.   Anna del Conte's Italian kitchen.
TX809.M17D437   1993
641.8'22—dc20   93–13291
                                                            CIP

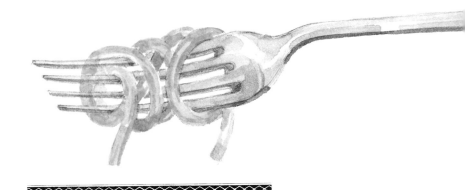

INTRODUCTION

Pasta is the simplest food, even simpler than bread, consisting only of semolina and water for dried pasta and flour and eggs for homemade pasta. It is also the food that can change its character and appearance more than any other, like some great character-actor, assuming countless different roles. Think of the golden lightness of a delicate dish of tagliatelle with butter and compare it with the intriguing, exotic flavor of a green dish of spaghetti with pesto, or the rich earthiness of a dish of baked lasagne. All are equally good in their different ways, and pasta is the main ingredient of them all.

TYPES OF PASTA

We Italians never look down on dried pasta. We consider it ideal for many sauces and would never regard it as merely a substitute for homemade pasta.

Factory-made **dried pasta** is made from durum wheat ground into semolina and mixed to a paste with water. The dough is forced through perforated metal disks to form the desired shape of pasta, and then dried. It should be buff-yellow, translucent, and slightly shiny. The most common kinds of dried pasta are spaghetti, long pasta of various widths and lengths, shapes such as fusilli, conchiglie, and penne, lasagne, and small pasta for soups.

The **"fresh pasta"** sold in specialist stores or supermarkets is made with durum wheat semolina, flour, eggs, and water. Though it is convenient, it certainly is not as good as homemade pasta, and it compares badly with dried pasta of a good Italian brand.

Homemade pasta has a lightness and delicacy that store-bought "fresh pasta" cannot match. So, when you want to make a recipe that calls for fresh pasta, do try to make it yourself, whether by hand or with the help of a machine. Remember, though, that it is not easy to make pasta by hand without practice, time, and a long, thin pasta rolling pin.

Luckily there are good machines to speed up the task. Some electric machines make good pasta, but they are expensive, noisy, and difficult to clean. The hand-cranked machines are cheap and easily obtained.

THE COOKING OF PASTA

The time pasta takes to cook differs according to its quality and shape, whether it is fresh or dried, and, of course, personal preference. Even in Italy, a plate of spaghetti that would be perfect in Naples might be considered undercooked in Milan. So I suggest you follow the table as a working guide.

COOKING TIMES FOR PASTA

Cooking time is calculated after the water returns to the boil

HOMEMADE PASTA	FRESH	DRIED
tagliatelle	1–2 minutes	2–3 minutes
tonnarelli	2–3 minutes	3–4 minutes
lasagne	2 minutes	4 minutes
stuffed shapes	5–6 minutes	7–9 minutes

As you can see from this chart, homemade pasta that has been left to dry takes longer to cook, as does store-bought fresh pasta

DRIED PASTA

capelli d'angelo	5 minutes
spaghettini	6–7 minutes
spaghetti, bigoli, long maccheroni, bucatini, linguine	8–10 minutes
tagliatelle	8–10 minutes
conchigliette or small tubular shapes	8 minutes
gnocchi, ditali, orecchiette, or any medium tubular shapes	8–10 minutes
penne, rigatoni, or any large tubular shapes	9–12 minutes

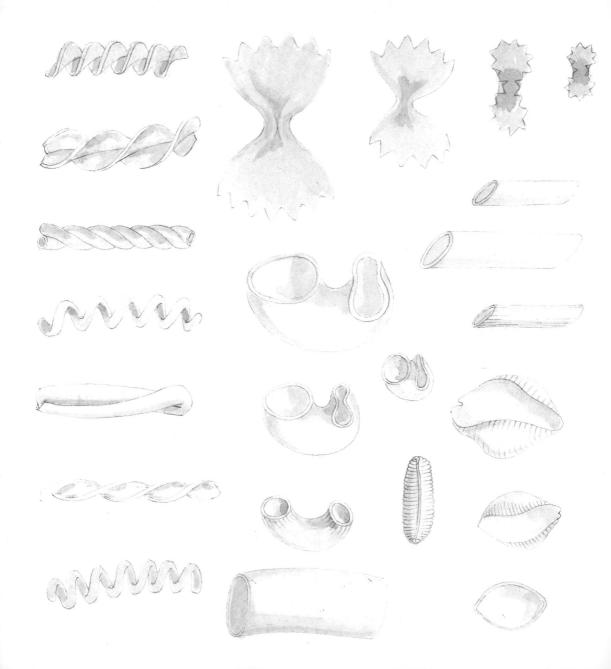

It is easy to cook pasta, but it can be spoiled by carelessness. Pasta needs to be cooked in a large saucepan and a lot of water – about 1 quart for $3\frac{1}{2}$ ounces of pasta. Bring the water to a boil and then add cooking salt – about $1\frac{1}{2}$ tablespoons for 4 quarts, which is the quantity needed for $\frac{3}{4}$ – 1 pound of pasta. The water might seem too salty, but it is thrown away and is not absorbed by the pasta.

Slide all the pasta into the boiling water, stir with a wooden fork or spoon to separate the pasta shapes, and cover the pan so that the water returns to a boil as soon as possible. Remove the lid and adjust the heat so that the water boils briskly, but does not boil over. The pasta is ready when it is *al dente*, which means that it offers some resistance to the bite. The best test to see if the pasta is ready is to take out a piece and pop it in your mouth. It is absolutely unnecessary to add cold water to pasta after cooking, as is sometimes suggested by non-Italian food writers.

THE AGNESI METHOD

When I went to Imperia many years ago to see over the Agnesi pasta factory, the late Vincenzo Agnesi told me the way he liked to cook pasta. Here is what I call the Agnesi method, which I find more suitable when I have friends to dinner, since the pasta does not become overcooked if you leave it a minute too long in the pot. It also produces a dish of pasta that retains the characteristic flavor of semolina. The method is only suitable for factory-dried pasta.

Bring a large saucepan of water to a boil, add salt to taste, and then add the pasta and stir. When the water has come back to a boil, cook 1 minute, stirring frequently. Remove from the heat, put a turkish towel over the pan, and close with a tight-fitting lid. Leave for the same length of time that the pasta would take to cook by the normal method, i.e. if it were still boiling. When the time is up, drain the pasta.

DRAINING PASTA

Pasta should be drained as soon as it is *al dente* (literally, "to the tooth"): you must be able to feel its texture when you bite into it. However, if the pasta is going to be cooked further, by baking or frying, drain it when it is still slightly undercooked. Pasta for salads should be even more *al dente*.

It is important to drain pasta properly. Use a colander that is large enough to contain all the pasta you have cooked, and that has three little feet to stand on in the sink. Tip the pasta in, give the colander two sharp shakes, and immediately turn the pasta into a heated bowl or dish, into the frying pan with the sauce, or into the saucepan in which it was cooked. (You can toss it better in the hot pan, with no worry about making a mess.) Penne, gnocchi, or any shapes that are hollow need more draining because water may be trapped in the hollows. However, pasta should never be overdrained, because it needs to be slippery for coating with the sauce. Do not leave it sitting "naked" in the colander, like the Chinese and Japanese do with their noodles. It should be dressed as soon as it is drained.

In southern Italy, they do not use a colander for long pasta. The spaghetti is lifted out of the pan with two long forks. It is kept in the air for only a few seconds for the excess water to run off and then immediately transferred to the frying pan or the serving bowl. The Neapolitans say *"Gli spaghetti devono avere la goccia"* – spaghetti must be still just dripping.

HOMEMADE PASTA

——— MAKING THE DOUGH ———

$1\frac{1}{3}$ cups, approximately, white flour (preferably Italian 00 – see below)
semolina flour for dusting
2 extra large eggs

Makes about $\frac{3}{4}$ pound pasta, enough for 4 people as a first course or 3 as a main course

Note: I recommend the use of Italian Grade 00 flour for making pasta dough. It is the best for this purpose because it absorbs the eggs more evenly, is easier to knead and roll out and, above all, makes pasta of a more fragrant flavour and a more delicate texture. Italian 00 flour is now available in most Italian specialist stores.

1 Put most of the flour on the work surface and make a well in the center. Place the rest of the flour to one side. Break the eggs into the well. Beat them lightly with a fork, about 1 minute, then draw the flour in gradually from the inner wall of the well. I do this with two fingers because I find that gives me more control. When the eggs are no longer runny, draw in enough flour to enable you to knead the dough. At this stage you might have to add the flour you set aside, and even a little more from the bag, which you should keep at hand. You should add enough flour so that the dough is no longer sticky. (It is not possible to give the exact amount of flour needed because it depends on the absorption capacity of the eggs and the humidity of the kitchen.) Work until the flour and eggs are thoroughly amalgamated, put the dough to one side and scrape the work surface clean. Wash and dry your hands.

Note: It is easier for a beginner to stretch a soft dough, though a dough that is too soft may stick and tear and become unmanageable. You can make a harder dough by replacing half the flour with fine semolina flour. This dough is difficult to roll out by hand, but it works all right in the hand-cranked machine. It makes a pasta that is less delicate and less smooth in texture, but with a definite flavor, particularly suitable for vegetable sauces.

2 Proceed to knead the dough by pressing and pushing with the heel of your palm, folding the dough back, giving it half a turn, and repeating these movements. Repeat the movements for about 10 minutes if you are going to make your pasta by hand, or 2–3 minutes if you are going to use a machine. Wrap the dough in plastic wrap and let it rest at least 30 minutes, though you can leave it up to 3 hours, or even overnight.

ROLLING OUT BY HAND

To roll out by hand you need, ideally, an Italian rolling pin, which is about 32 inches long and $1\frac{1}{2}$ inches in diameter. If you do not have a *mattarello* – long, thin rolling pin – you must divide the dough and roll it out in two batches, so that the circle of rolled-out pasta does not become too large for your rolling pin.

ROLLING OUT BY MACHINE

I still think the hand-cranked machine is the best machine to use, and worth every penny of its very reasonable price. This is how to proceed.

Unwrap the dough and lightly dust the work surface with flour. Knead the dough, as before, a further 2 minutes, then divide it into four equal parts. Take one piece of dough and carefully re-wrap the other pieces in plastic wrap.

Set the rollers of the machine to the widest opening. Flatten the piece of dough slightly, so that it nearly reaches the width of the machine. Run it through the machine five or six times, folding the sheet over and giving it a 180° turn each time. When the dough is smooth, run the sheet, unfolded and without turning it, through all the settings, closing the rollers one notch at a time until you achieve the desired thickness. For good results it is very important that you push the sheet of dough through each setting. If the sheet tears or sticks to the machine, dust it on both sides with flour.

For tonnarelli (like spaghetti but square in section), stop the rolling out at the second from last setting. For tagliatelle or tagliolini.

stop at the last but one. For flat sheet pasta, stop at the last setting. If the atmosphere is damp, dough rolled out too thin cannot be stuffed to make ravioli or other small shapes because, instead of drying, it becomes more and more soggy when filled with the stuffing. If you find this happening, stop rolling out at the last but one setting. Alternatively, I sometimes prefer to roll out the strip twice through the last but one setting. This makes the pasta just a little thinner, but not as thin as the last setting. Roll out the dough to the last setting only for lasagne or cannelloni.

FOR LONG PASTA, TAGLIATELLE, FETTUCCINE, TONNARELLI, TAGLIOLINI

Lay each sheet of pasta dough on a clean dish towel, letting about one-third of its length hang down over the edge of the work surface. Leave until the pasta is dry to the touch and slightly leathery, but still pliable. This process takes about 30 minutes, depending on the humidity of the atmosphere and the texture of the pasta, and is essential because it prevents the strands from sticking together. Feed each sheet through the broad cutters of the machine for tagliatelle or fettuccine, or through the narrow ones for tonnarelli or tagliolini.

Separate the cut strands or wind them

loosely around your hand to make nests. Spread them out on clean dish cloths, and lightly dust them with semolina flour. Do not use all-purpose flour because this would be absorbed into the dough. The pasta is now ready to be cooked, or it can be dried and then stored in an airtight tin or plastic bag. Be very careful how you handle it because dried homemade pasta is very brittle and breaks easily.

LASAGNE AND CANNELLONI

Proceed immediately to cut the shapes without drying the sheets. Cut each pasta sheet into squares of about $3\frac{1}{2} \times 5$ inches for lasagne, or 3×4 inches for cannelloni.

PAPPARDELLE

Roll out each sheet of pasta to the last but one notch of the hand-cranked machine. Leave the sheets to dry no longer than 10 minutes and then cut into ribbons about 5 to 6 inches long and $\frac{3}{4}$ inch wide. Lay the pappardelle, not touching each other, on clean dish towels.

STUFFED PASTA SHAPES

You must work right away while the pasta dough is still fresh and pliable. Roll out the dough and stuff the sheets, one or two at a time, depending on the shape being made. Keep the remainder of the dough in plastic wrap.

Cook the little shapes immediately or leave them until the next day, spread out on a clean cloth, dusted with semolina flour. Once dry, you can store stuffed pasta in plastic boxes, in layers interleaved with wax paper. Do not keep them longer than a day or the stuffing might be spoiled.

GREEN PASTA

The only colored pasta I consider worth writing about is the traditional green pasta made with spinach. All the modern creations of red, black, or brown pasta are gimmicks, and sometimes they spoil the flavor of the pasta. Flavor and color should be added only by the sauce.

$\frac{3}{4}$ cup cooked fresh spinach, or frozen spinach, thawed and cooked 5 minutes
$1\frac{1}{2}$ cups white flour, preferably Italian 00
2 extra large eggs

Squeeze all the liquid out of the spinach with your hands. Chop it very finely with a knife. Do not use a food processor because the spinach would become like a liquid mass. Add the chopped spinach to the well in the flour together with the eggs, and knead and roll out as for normal pasta.

SAUCES FOR SHAPES

In Italy, there are said to be 350 different shapes of pasta (I've never counted them!). Although you are unlikely to find such a vast number of pasta shapes outside Italy, there are now a very considerable number to choose from. The drawings on pages 6–7 are of the most common and easily available shapes. In the recipes I explain which shape of pasta is usually dressed with the sauce in question, but you do not have to follow my suggestions slavishly.

There are, however, certain basic rules that govern which pasta shapes should be dressed with which sauce. In general, long, thin shapes are dressed with an olive-oil-based sauce that allows the strands to remain slippery and separate. Typical recipes are spaghettini with oil, garlic, and chili (page 20) and the spaghetti with tomato sauce on page 19.

Thicker long shapes, such as ziti, tonnarelli, bucatini, or fettuccine, are best in heavier sauces containing prosciutto or bits of meat, cheese, and eggs. A prime example is the carbonara on page 37.

Medium-size short tubular pasta like ditali, orecchiette, and fusilli are perfect with vegetable sauces of any kind, these being the shapes traditionally made in southern Italy, where pasta is most often combined with vegetables.

Penne and maccheroni and other large tubular shapes, as well as homemade shapes such as garganelli and pappardelle, are the perfect foil for a rich meat *ragù* and for use in most baked dishes. A *ragù* bolognese is traditionally combined with tagliatelle, and the choice for a northern Italian pasta al gratin (page 48) is penne.

As for the proportion of sauce to pasta, an average of 2 generous spoonsful of well-reduced sauce per portion of pasta is a good general guide.

―――― ARRANGEMENT OF RECIPES ――――

The recipes in this book are grouped according to the main ingredient of the sauce. Thus tagliatelle with bolognese sauce will be found with other recipes whose sauces are based on fish and meat products, while penne with tomato sauce is with the other recipes for vegetable-based sauces, such as orecchiette with broccoli.

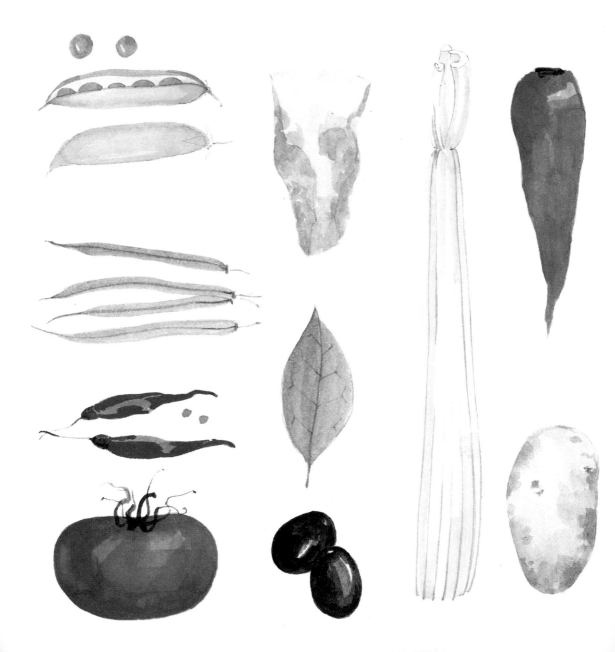

PASTA WITH VEGETABLE SAUCES

PESTO
PESTO SAUCE

⅓ cup pine nuts
3 ounces fresh basil leaves
(about 2 cups)
1 garlic clove, peeled
pinch of rock salt
¼ cup freshly grated Parmesan
cheese
2 tablespoons freshly grated
aged romano cheese
6 tablespoons extra virgin
olive oil
3 tablespoons unsalted butter

U se young basil leaves for pesto: Basil that has been growing too long acquires an unpleasantly strong taste. The pine nuts must be fresh, i.e. of the current year, and the oil must be a very good olive oil, although an unassertive one. If possible use an oil from Liguria or from Lake Garda (they can be found in specialist shops); they are less pungent than a Tuscan oil, and less herby than an oil from Apulia.

The oil must be added slowly, as for mayonnaise, so as to create the right thickness. Some cooks add walnuts as well as pine nuts, but I prefer to add only pine nuts in order to keep the emphasis on the fresh flavor of the basil. If you have time, make your pesto by hand in a mortar; More juices are released than would be by the chopping action of the metal blade in a food processor or blender. I add a little softened butter to the pesto just before serving, to make the sauce sweeter and more delicate. Before tossing the pesto with the pasta, always dilute it with 3 or 4 tablespoons of the water in which the pasta has been cooking.

1 Heat the oven to 350°F. Spread the pine nuts on a baking sheet and toast in the oven 5 minutes or so. This will bring out the flavor of the nuts.

2 To make in a mortar:
Put the basil leaves, garlic, pine nuts, and salt in the mortar. Grind against the sides of the mortar with the pestle, crushing the ingredients until the mixture has become a paste. Mix in the grated cheeses. Add the oil gradually, beating with a wooden spoon.

To make in a food processor or blender:
Cut the garlic into thin slices and drop them into the container of

the food processor or blender. Add the basil, pine nuts, salt, and oil and process to a creamy consistency. Transfer the sauce to a bowl and mix in the cheeses.

3 Melt the butter over the lowest heat and blend into the pesto.

Pesto freezes very well. Omit the garlic and the cheeses and add them just before you are going to use the sauce.

PICAGGE AL PESTO

PICAGGE WITH PESTO SAUCE

I n Liguria, the motherland of pesto, potato and a handful of green beans are cooked with the pasta. The pasta I like to use with pesto is picagge, meaning ribbons. Picagge are half the width of lasagne, but the same length.

1 Cut the pasta dough into strips about 2 × 5 inches. You can cut this shape as soon as you have rolled it out; you do not have to let the pasta dry.

2 Cook the potatoes in their skins in boiling salted water. Drain, then peel and slice them. Put in a bowl.

3 Trim the beans. Cook them in plenty of boiling salted water until tender and then drain. Add to the potatoes. Toss with 3 or 4 tablespoons of the pesto.

4 Cook the pasta in plenty of boiling salted water until *al dente*. Drain, reserving a cupful of the water, and return to the pan. Add 2 or 3 tablespoons of the water to the pesto.

5 Toss the pasta with half the pesto. Transfer half the pasta to a heated serving dish. Spoon over the potato and bean mixture and cover with the rest of the pasta. Spread the remaining pesto on top.

Homemade pasta keeps well in a hot oven for 15 minutes or so.

Serves 4 as a main course

homemade pasta dough, made with 3 extra large eggs and $2\frac{1}{4}$ cups flour (page 9), or 1 pound 2 ounces bought linguine or fettuccine
3 small new potatoes
$\frac{1}{2}$ pound young green beans
pesto sauce from the preceeding recipe

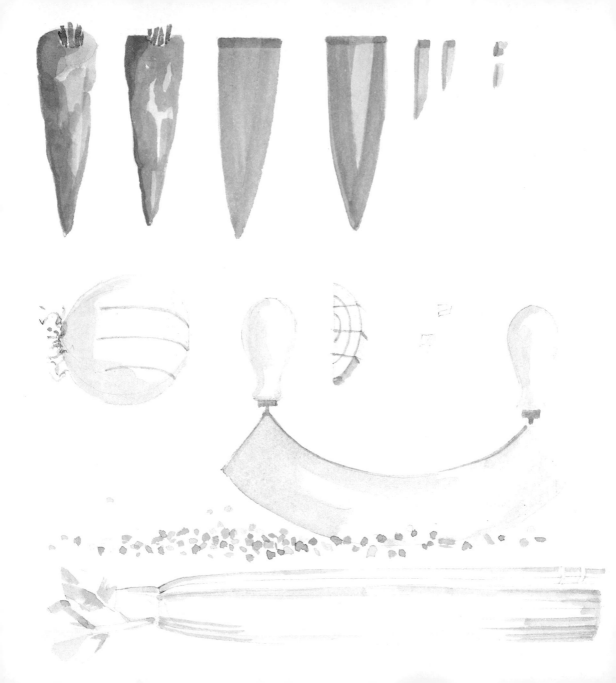

PASTA AL SUGO

PASTA WITH TOMATO SAUCE

The first tomato sauce here is denser and darker than the second one because of the many sautéed vegetables. It is suitable for most dried pasta.

1 Sauté the onion, carrot, and celery in the olive oil over low heat until well softened; this will take at least 10 minutes. Add the garlic and chili pepper just a few minutes before you finish the *soffritto* (sautéed mixture).

2 Add the chopped tomatoes, the herbs, and sugar. Season lightly with salt and pepper.

3 Simmer gently over low heat, uncovered, until the oil begins to separate into small drops around the edge, 30–40 minutes. Stir occasionally to prevent the sauce sticking to the bottom.

4 Remove and discard the parsley stems and bay leaf, and push the sauce through the coarsest disk of a vegetable mill. Put the sauce in a small saucepan. When the pasta is nearly ready, heat up the sauce.

5 Cook the pasta in plenty of boiling salted water until *al dente*. Drain well and toss with the sauce. Serve at once, and pass a bowl of freshly grated Parmesan cheese separately.

A simpler and fresher tomato sauce can be made in the summer when good fresh tomatoes are on the market. Peel, seed and coarsely chop 2lb of ripe tomatoes and put them in a large heavy-bottomed sauté pan with 5 tbsp extra virgin olive oil, 6 garlic cloves, bruised, salt and freshly ground black pepper, a dozen snipped fresh basil leaves or $\frac{1}{2}$ tbsp of dried oregano. Cook briskly for 5 minutes, stirring frequently, until a lot of the tomato water has evaporated. Remove and discard the garlic before serving.

Serves 6 as a first course or 4 as a main course

1 medium-size onion,
very finely chopped
1 medium-size carrot,
very finely chopped
1 celery stalk,
very finely chopped
$\frac{1}{4}$ cup olive oil
1 garlic clove, minced
1 small dried chili pepper,
seeded and chopped (optional)
$3\frac{1}{2}$ cups canned Italian plum
tomatoes, coarsely chopped
4 parsley stems
1 bay leaf
1 teaspoon dried oregano
1 teaspoon sugar
salt and freshly ground
black pepper
1 pound 2 ounces tubular pasta,
such as penne or rigatoni
freshly grated Parmesan
cheese, for serving

SPAGHETTINI AGLIO OLIO E PEPERONCINO

—— THIN SPAGHETTI WITH OIL, GARLIC, AND CHILI ——

Serves 4 as a first course or
3 as a main course

$\frac{3}{4}$ pound thin spaghetti
(spaghettini)
salt
$\frac{1}{2}$ cup extra virgin olive oil
3 garlic cloves, sliced
1 or 2 small dried chili peppers,
according to taste, seeded and
crumbled

This sauce differs from that in Tagliatelle with Butter and Parmesan (page 52), in a way that demonstrates the essential difference between the cooking of northern Italy and that of the South. The aggressive flavor of the dish here shows all the characteristics of Mediterranean cooking, while the delicate, but certainly not bland, Tagliatelle with Butter epitomizes northern Italian cooking with its abundant use of butter and Parmesan.

1 Cook the pasta in plenty of boiling salted water, remembering that spaghettini will cook in about 6 minutes.
2 Meanwhile, put the oil, garlic, and chilies in a frying pan large enough to hold all the pasta later. Cook over low heat until the garlic aroma rises, about 1 minute. Immediately remove the pan from the heat or the garlic might burn: This would ruin the taste of the oil.
3 Drain the pasta as soon as it is *al dente*. Do not overcook it. Transfer the pasta immediately to the frying pan. Stir-fry a minute or so, using two forks and lifting the spaghettini high into the air so that every strand is beautifully glistening with oil. Serve at once, preferably straight from the pan.

No cheese is needed for this typically Neapolitan quick pasta.

PAPARELE E BISI

TAGLIATELLE WITH PEAS

"Paparele" and *"bisi"* are the Venetian dialect words for wide tagliatelle and *piselli*, peas, which are one of the Venetians' favorite vegetables. Here, they are used to dress fresh tagliatelle in a delicate, well-balanced sauce. The sauce is also suitable for dressing a dish of dried farfalle.

1 Put half the butter, the pancetta, and onion in a small saucepan and sauté until the onion is soft and golden.

2 Mix in the peas and parsley and then pour in the broth. Stir and add salt and pepper to taste. Cover the pan and cook over very low heat until the peas are tender. The sauce should be quite thin.

3 Meanwhile, cook the pasta in plenty of boiling salted water until it is *al dente*. Drain and return to the pan.

4 Toss the pasta with the rest of the butter. Pour the sauce over the pasta and mix in the Parmesan.

Serves 6 as a first course or 4 as a main course

4 tablespoons butter
2 ounces unsmoked pancetta, chopped
1 tablespoon finely chopped onion
2 cups cooked green peas, or frozen petite peas, thawed
1 tablespoon chopped fresh flat-leaf Italian parsley
$\frac{1}{2}$ cup beef broth
salt and freshly ground black pepper
homemade tagliatelle, made with 3 extra large eggs and $2\frac{1}{4}$ cups flour (page 9), or 1 pound 2 ounces bought fresh tagliatelle
$\frac{1}{2}$ cup freshly grated Parmesan cheese

ORECCHIETTE CON I BROCCOLI
PASTA WITH BROCCOLI

Serves 4 as a first course or 3 as a main course

1 pound broccoli
salt and freshly ground black pepper
$\frac{3}{4}$ pound orecchiette or other medium-size pasta, or whole-wheat spaghetti
2 garlic cloves, peeled
1 small dried chili pepper, seeded
3 salted anchovies, boned and rinsed, or 6 canned anchovy fillets, drained
6 tablespoons extra virgin olive oil
$\frac{1}{4}$ cup freshly grated aged romano cheese

The combination of vegetables and pasta has its origins in Southern Italy. In Apulia, this broccoli sauce is always served with orecchiette, which means "little ears" because of their hollow shape. Orecchiette are made at home there, with semolina, flour, and water. They are now produced commercially by the best Italian pasta manufacturers and are generally available within Italy and elsewhere.

I find that this sauce, as well as being good with orecchiette, is also one of the few that can stand up to the nutty flavor of brown pasta made with whole-wheat flour (a flavor of which, like most Italians, I am not particularly fond). Whole-wheat pasta is made in a number of shapes, among which spaghetti is by far the most successful.

1 Trim the broccoli. Divide into small florets and cut the stems into 1-inch rounds.

2 Bring a large saucepan of water to a boil. Add about $1\frac{1}{2}$ tablespoons of cooking salt and then slide in the broccoli. Stir well and, when the water has come back to a boil, cook 5 minutes. Retrieve the broccoli from the water with a slotted spoon and lay them on paper towels. Pat dry and set aside.

3 Bring the broccoli water back to a boil and add the pasta. Cook in the usual way until very *al dente*.

4 While the pasta is cooking, chop the garlic, chili pepper, and anchovy fillets together and sauté them in half the oil for 2 minutes, using a large frying pan. Mix in the broccoli and sauté for a few minutes, turning constantly.

5 When the pasta is done, drain and turn it into the frying pan. Stir-fry a minute, then taste and check the seasoning.

6 Before you serve the pasta, add the rest of the olive oil and mix in the romano. If you like, you can serve a bowl of freshly grated Parmesan cheese on the side, although I find that the romano gives the dish enough of a cheesey taste.

TAGLIATELLE COL SUGO DI FUNGHI
TAGLIATELLE WITH MUSHROOM SAUCE

Serves 6 as a first course or
4 as a main course

1 ounce dried porcini
1 pound mixed fresh
mushrooms: such as common
mushrooms and oyster
mushrooms
5 tablespoons butter
4 shallots, very finely chopped
salt and freshly ground
black pepper
1 garlic clove, minced
1 tablespoon chopped
fresh parsley
1 tablespoon chopped fresh
marjoram, or 2 teaspoons dried
marjoram
2 teaspoons tomato paste
1 tablespoon flour
1 cup beef broth
$\frac{2}{3}$ cup dry white wine
about $\frac{1}{4}$ of a nutmeg, grated
homemade tagliatelle, made
with 3 extra large eggs and $2\frac{1}{4}$
cups flour (page 9), or $1\frac{1}{2}$
pounds bought fresh tagliatelle
freshly grated Parmesan
cheese, for serving (optional)

I have adapted an old family recipe to suit the mushrooms that are available in this country. Admittedly there are more and more species of mushrooms in the shops, but they are not equally available in all parts of the country. The other reason why I have adapted the Italian recipe is that the sauce is so good that I want to be able to make it at any time of the year, and not only when the wild mushrooms are in season.

The woody, leafy perfume of cèpes (porcini) is given here by the dried porcini, which you can easily buy in Italian specialist stores and many supermarkets. To these you add a selection of cultivated mushrooms for a sweeter flavor and for texture.

1 Put the dried porcini in a bowl and cover with very hot water. Let soak 30 minutes or so and then lift them out. If they still have some grit, rinse under cold water. Dry and chop them. Filter the liquid through a cheesecloth-lined strainer and reserve.
2 Clean the fresh mushrooms by wiping them with damp paper towels. If they are very dirty, rinse them under cold water. Dry and chop them coarsely. (I use a food processor which I pulsate for only a few seconds.)
3 Put half the butter and the shallots in a large sauté pan, add a pinch of salt, and cook until the shallots are soft. Stir in the garlic and herbs and sauté a further minute. Add the tomato paste and cook 30 seconds. Add the dried porcini and sauté 5 minutes and then add the fresh mushrooms. Sauté over medium heat 5 minutes, turning the mushrooms over and over to *insaporire* – take up the flavor. Season with a little more salt and with a generous grinding of pepper. Turn the heat down and cook a further 5 minutes.
4 Melt the remaining butter in a heavy-bottomed saucepan and

blend in the flour. Add the broth, stirring constantly and hard until well blended.

5 Heat the wine and add to the butter and stock mixture together with the nutmeg. Add some of the filtered porcini liquid, just enough to add mushroom flavor to the sauce, but not too much because it can be overpowering. Continue cooking over very low heat about 15 minutes. Stir in the mushroom mixture. Check the seasoning and cook over the lowest possible heat about 10 minutes.

6 Meanwhile, cook the tagliatelle in plenty of boiling salted water until *al dente*. Drain, but do not overdrain, reserving a cupful of the pasta water.

7 Turn half the pasta into a heated bowl and toss with half the mushroom sauce. Cover with the rest of the pasta and mix in the remaining sauce. If the pasta seems too dry, add 2–3 tablespoons of the reserved water. Remember that fresh pasta absorbs a lot of liquid while it is sitting in the bowl. Serve at once with the optional cheese.

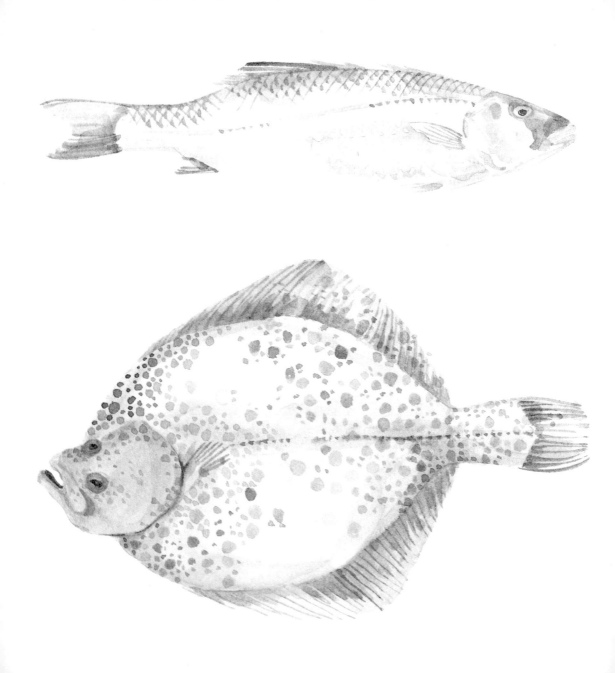

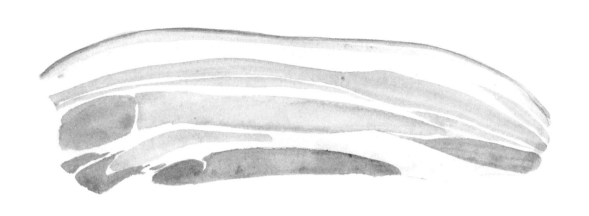

PASTA WITH
MEAT & FISH
SAUCES

TONNARELLI ALLA PURE DI TONNO
—— TONNARELLI WITH TUNA AND ANCHOVY PURÉE ——

Serves 4 as a first course or
3 as a main course

7 ounces canned Italian or
Spanish tuna packed in olive oil,
drained
$1\frac{1}{2}$ salted anchovies,
boned and rinsed, or
3 canned anchovy fillets
3 tablespoons pine nuts
3 tablespoons freshly grated
Parmesan cheese
salt and freshly ground
black pepper
$\frac{1}{4}$ cup extra virgin olive oil

homemade tonnarelli, made with
2 extra large eggs and $1\frac{1}{3}$ cups
flour (page 9), or $\frac{3}{4}$ pound
bought fresh tagliatelle

"There she goes again!" they say, when I hold forth about canned tuna. In most supermarkets the tuna on sale is skipjack tuna fish, an inferior fish, smaller in size and coarser in taste than the Mediterranean tuna. I strongly advise you to buy Italian or Spanish tuna packed in olive oil, which is available in most speciality stores. It is more expensive, but it is a very superior product. And it is absolutely necessary for this delicate creamy sauce.

Tonnarelli are a kind of square homemade pasta, particularly suitable for a smooth fish sauce.

1 Put the tuna, anchovies, pine nuts, cheese, and pepper to taste in a food processor. Process while gradually adding the olive oil.
2 Slide the pasta into a saucepan of boiling water, to which only 1 tablespoon salt has been added. (The sauce is quite salty.) Cook until *al dente*.
3 Scoop out a cupful of the pasta water and add about 6 tablespoons of it to the sauce through the hole in the lid of the processor. The sauce should have the consistency of a thin béchamel. Taste and check the pepper.
4 Drain the tonnarelli and turn it into a heated bowl. Pour the sauce over it and toss thoroughly. Serve immediately.

BUCATINI ALL'AMATRICIANA
BUCATINI WITH SMOKED PANCETTA AND
TOMATO SAUCE

A matrice is a town on the central Apennines where on August 15th, huge cauldrons of this dish are prepared for the local *festa*. The sauce is traditionally made with pork jowl, and flavored with a lot of dried chili pepper and grated romano to counterbalance the fattiness of the meat. Outside of Italy, I use smoked pancetta, which I buy in a thick piece.

1 Put the pancetta and oil in a non-stick frying pan and sauté until the pancetta fat has been rendered and the pancetta is crisp and browned. Stir frequently.

2 Add the onion and a pinch of salt to the frying pan and sauté about 10 minutes longer. Mix in the garlic and chili pepper. Cook a further minute or so and then splash in the wine. Turn the heat up and let the wine bubble away to reduce it by half. Pour in the tomato sauce and simmer 15 minutes to let the flavors combine. Add salt and add pepper to your liking.

3 Cook the bucatini in plenty of boiling salted water until *al dente*. Drain thoroughly, giving the colander a few sharp shakes so that the water trapped in the bucatini comes out. Transfer the pasta to a heated bowl and mix in three-quarters of the sauce and the romano. Toss very thoroughly and then spoon over the rest of the sauce. Serve immediately, passing the Parmesan separately in a bowl.

Serves 6 as a first course or
4 as a main course

$\frac{3}{4}$ pound smoked pancetta,
cut into $\frac{1}{2}$-inch cubes
1 tablespoon olive oil
1 small onion, very finely
chopped
salt and freshly ground
black pepper
1 garlic clove, minced
1 small dried chili pepper,
seeded and finely chopped
$\frac{1}{2}$ cup dry white wine
2 cups tomato sauce (page 19,
bottom)
1 pound bucatini
6 tablespoons freshly grated
aged romano cheese
freshly grated Parmesan
cheese, for serving

TAGLIOLINI VERDI COL SALMONE E I FUNGHI

GREEN TAGLIOLINI WITH A SALMON AND
MUSHROOM SAUCE

Serves 3 or 4

$\frac{3}{4}$ ounce dried porcini
$\frac{3}{4}$ pound piece of fresh salmon
1 cup fish or vegetable broth
$\frac{1}{2}$ cup dry white wine
5 tablespoons unsalted butter
1 shallot, very finely chopped
salt and freshly ground
black pepper
6 ounces fresh common
mushrooms, cleaned and
coarsely chopped
$1\frac{1}{2}$ tablespoons flour
3 tablespoons whipping cream
homemade green tagliolini,
made with 2 extra large eggs,
$1\frac{1}{2}$ cups flour and $\frac{3}{4}$ cup cooked
or frozen spinach (page 9), or
1 pound bought green tagliolini
bunch of fresh dill, chopped
freshly grated Parmesan
cheese, for serving

I n no way can I claim this to be a traditional Italian dish. It is an Anna Del Conte invention, good enough to pass on. It is definitely a *piatto unico* (one-course meal), with a good salad to be served afterward, but not with it.

1 Put the dried porcini in a small bowl and cover with very hot water. Let soak about 30 minutes.
2 Meanwhile, put the salmon in a saucepan and cover with the broth and wine. Bring to a boil and boil 1 minute. Remove from the heat and leave the salmon in the pan to finish cooking while you start the sauce.
3 Put half the butter and the shallot in a heavy-bottomed sauce-pan. Sprinkle with salt and cook gently until the shallot is soft, stirring occasionally.

4 Lift the porcini out of the soaking water. If they are very dirty, rinse them under cold water. Dry and chop them coarsely. Filter the porcini liquid through a strainer lined with cheesecloth to catch any grit, and reserve.

5 Add the chopped porcini to the shallot and sauté 5 minutes over low heat. Mix in the fresh mushrooms, turn the heat up, and cook until the liquid has come out of the mushrooms. Stir frequently.

6 Lift the fish out of the broth and place it on a board. Strain the broth and reserve.

7 Blend the flour into the mushroom sauce and cook a minute or so, stirring constantly. Pour over a cupful of the fish broth and stir rapidly over very low heat until smoothly blended. Add the rest of the broth very gradually, stirring constantly. Add 2–3 tablespoons of the filtered porcini liquid. The sauce should be quite thin.

8 Bring the sauce slowly to a boil, then turn the heat right down, so that only a few bubbles break the surface of the sauce every now and then, and cook 30 minutes. I use a flame-tamer. Alternatively you can cook the sauce in a water bath: Place the pan containing the sauce in another saucepan of gently simmering water. You can, of course, simmer your mushroom sauce only 5 minutes, but you will not achieve the same velvety, delicate yet rich sauce. At the end, mix in the cream. Taste and adjust the seasoning.

9 Skin and bone the fish and flake the flesh. Add to the sauce and keep warm.

10 Cook the tagliolini in plenty of boiling salted water until *al dente*. Drain and return them to the hot saucepan in which they cooked. Toss with the remaining butter. Transfer to a heated bowl and cover with the sauce. Sprinkle the dill over the top just before serving. Pass the grated Parmesan in a bowl.

TAGLIATELLE AL RAGU
─────── TAGLIATELLE WITH BOLOGNESE SAUCE ───────

Serves 6 as a first course or
4 as a main course

For the bolognese sauce
2 tablespoons butter
3 tablespoons extra virgin olive
oil
2 ounces unsmoked pancetta or
bacon, finely chopped
1 small onion, finely chopped
$\frac{1}{2}$ carrot, finely chopped
1 celery stalk, finely chopped
1 garlic clove, minced
1 bay leaf
$\frac{3}{4}$ pound ground chuck or round
1 tablespoon tomato paste
$\frac{2}{3}$ cup red wine
$\frac{2}{3}$ cup beef broth
2 pinches of grated nutmeg
salt and freshly ground
black pepper
homemade tagliatelle, made
with 3 extra large eggs and $2\frac{1}{4}$
cups flour (page 9) or $1\frac{1}{2}$
pounds bought fresh tagliatelle
freshly grated Parmesan
cheese, for serving

Bolognese sauce is out of fashion. A great pity, although I quite understand why.

The early emigrants from southern Italy to the USA took their beloved spaghetti with them. In America, when they opened their restaurants, they realized that the locals were great meat lovers. Thus, instead of introducing spaghetti with the traditional tomato sauce, the Italians had the clever idea – financially clever, but not gastronomically – of serving spaghetti with a meat sauce or meat balls. The meat sauce was a watered-down version, both literally and figuratively, of the *ragù bolognese*.

It quickly caught on, and spaghetti bolognese became synonymous with Italian cooking. But in fact there is no combination of pasta and sauce that is less typically Italian!

In Bologna, *ragù* is used to dress the local pasta – tagliatelle, not spaghetti – fresh, homemade with eggs and local soft-wheat flour. And what a wonderful dish it is. If you cannot afford the time to make your own tagliatelle, choose good fresh pasta. Remember that dried egg tagliatelle made by a reputable Italian producer are often better than fresh pasta made with inferior flour, a minimum of eggs, and a lot of water.

1 To make the bolognese sauce, heat the butter and oil in a heavy-bottomed saucepan and cook the pancetta 2 minutes, stirring constantly.

2 Add the onion, and, when it has begun to soften, add the carrot, celery, garlic, and bay leaf. Cook 10 minutes longer, stirring frequently.

3 Put in the ground beef and cook to brown it as much as possible, crumbling it in the pan with a fork. Do this over high heat so that the meat browns rather than stews.

4 Add the tomato paste and continue to cook over high heat 2 minutes longer. Still over high heat, splash in the wine and boil to evaporate. Remove and discard the bay leaf and pour in the broth. Season with the nutmeg, salt, and pepper. Mix well and simmer, uncovered, about 2 hours. Stir occasionally and add a little hot water if the sauce is too dry. The ragù should cook very slowly indeed, at the lowest possible simmer.

5 Cook the pasta in plenty of boiling salted water. Fresh pasta cooks quickly, so stay around and test after $1\frac{1}{2}$ minutes. Drain as soon as it is *al dente*, reserving a cupful of the pasta water.

6 Return half the pasta to the hot saucepan and stir in about half the *ragù*. Pour in the rest of the tagliatelle and the rest of the *ragù*. Mix very well, adding 2–3 tablespoons of the reserved water if the pasta seems dry. Transfer to a heated bowl or deep dish and serve immediately, passing the cheese separately.

PASTA CON LE SARDE

PASTA WITH FRESH SARDINES

Serves 4 as a main course

½ cup currants
6 tablespoons extra virgin
olive oil
1 red or Bermuda onion, very
finely sliced
salt and freshly ground
black pepper
¼ cup pine nuts
7 ounces wild or cultivated
fennel leaves
2 salted anchovies,
boned and rinsed, or
4 canned anchovy fillets
1 pound fresh sardines, boned
(see Note opposite)
1 teaspoon fennel seeds
¾ pound bucatini

This dish from Sicily is like a history of that island in microcosm: part Greek, part Saracen, part Norman. The sardines and wild fennel, typical food of the ancient Greeks, are here used to dress the most Italian of all foods, pasta. The dressing is lightened and made more interesting by the inclusion of pine nuts and currants, a Saracen influence, and the finished dish is cooked in the oven, a method brought to the island by the Normans. If you cannot get hold of wild or cultivated fennel leaves, use a small fennel bulb, cut into strips, together with its feathery green top.

1 Soak the currants in warm water 10 minutes. Drain and dry well with paper towels.

2 Put 2 tablespoons of the oil in a frying pan, add the onion and a pinch of salt, and sauté over low heat, stirring frequently, until soft, about 15 minutes. Mix in the currants and pine nuts and cook a further 2 minutes.

3 Meanwhile, blanch the fennel leaves in a large saucepan of boiling salted water for 1 minute. (If you are using fennel bulb, cook until soft.) Lift the fennel out of the water with a slotted spoon, drain, and dry with paper towels. Reserve the water in which it has cooked. Chop the fennel and add to the onion mixture. Cook over very low heat 10–15 minutes, adding 2–3 tablespoons of the fennel water whenever the mixture appears too dry.

4 Heat the oven to 400°F.

5 Chop about half the sardines and the anchovies and add to the pan with the fennel seeds and a generous grinding of pepper. Cook gently 10 minutes, stirring frequently and adding more fennel water whenever necessary. Taste and adjust the seasoning.

6 Heat 2 tablespoons of the remaining oil in a nonstick frying pan. When the oil is very hot, but not yet smoking, slide in the remaining whole sardines and fry on both sides, about 5 minutes.
7 Meanwhile, cook the pasta in the fennel water until very *al dente*. Drain, return the pasta to the pan, and dress immediately with the sardine sauce.
8 Grease a baking dish with a little oil and transfer the pasta to it. Lay the fried sardines over the pasta, dribble with the rest of the oil, and cover with foil. Bake 15 minutes.

The dish can be prepared a few hours in advance and then baked an extra 15 minutes to heat the pasta through.

Note: To clean and bone fresh sardines, snap off the head of each fish and pull it away, thus removing most of the inside. Remove the back fin by pulling it off, starting from the tail end. Hold the sardine with one hand and open the belly with the thumb of the other hand, running it against the spine on both sides. Open the fish, butterfly-fashion, and pull the spine sharply from the head end toward the tail end, giving a last sharp tug to remove the tail. Wash and dry the boned fish.

PAPPARDELLE CON LA LEPRE
PAPPARDELLE WITH HARE

Serves 5 or 6 as a main course

2 tablespoons olive oil
5 tablespoons unsalted butter
1 ounce unsmoked pancetta, chopped
1 small onion, very finely chopped
1 small celery stick, very finely chopped
1 garlic clove, minced
a small sprig of fresh rosemary, finely chopped
the legs of 1 hare
$\frac{2}{3}$ cup red wine
2 teaspoons flour
$\frac{2}{3}$ cup beef broth
salt and freshly ground black pepper
pinch of grated nutmeg
2 tablespoons whipping cream
homemade pappardelle, made with 3 extra large eggs and $2\frac{1}{4}$ cups flour (page 9), or 14 ounces dried tagliatelle, or 1 pound 2 ounces bought fresh tagliatelle

Only the legs of the hare are used for this dish. You can roast the saddle as they do in Tuscany, which is where this dish originally comes from. It is a rich dish, and is regarded as a *piatto unico* – one-course meal – even in Italy, where pasta is usually only the first course.

1 Heat the oil and half the butter in a sauté pan and cook the pancetta for 2 minutes, stirring constantly. Add the onion and sauté 5 minutes longer, stirring very frequently. Add the celery, garlic, and rosemary and cook until soft. Push the *soffritto* to one side of the pan.

2 Add the hare legs and brown well on all sides. Raise the heat, pour in the wine, and boil until the liquid has reduced by half.

3 Transfer the hare to a plate. Stir the flour into the cooking juices. Cook 1 minute and then pour in half the broth. Mix well. Return the hare to the pan and season with salt and nutmeg. Turn the heat down to very low and cook gently about 1 hour, with the lid slightly askew. If the sauce gets too dry, add a little of the remaining broth. The sauce should in the end be quite thick.

4 Remove the hare from the pan. Bone the legs and cut the meat into very small pieces. Return the meat to the pan and add the cream and pepper to taste. Cook about 2 minutes, stirring constantly. Taste and adjust the seasoning, then remove from the heat. Reheat the sauce before adding to the pasta.

5 Cook the pasta in plenty of boiling salted water until *al dente*, remembering that if you are using fresh homemade pasta it will only take about 1 minute to cook. Drain and turn the pasta into a heated bowl. Add the remaining butter and spoon the hot hare sauce on top. Serve at once.

SPAGHETTI ALLA CARBONARA
SPAGHETTI WITH EGGS AND BACON

The creation of this dish is attributed to the *carbonari* – charcoal burners – who used to make their charcoal in the mountainous forests of Lazio. Traditionally, the meat used was the jowl of the pig, but nowadays most carbonara is made with pancetta, which is belly of pork, similar to bacon but differently cured.

1 Heat the oil, sage leaves, and garlic clove in a large frying pan. Add the pancetta and sauté until the pancetta is golden brown and the fat has been rendered, about 10 minutes. Discard the garlic and sage.

2 Cook the spaghetti in plenty of boiling salted water until *al dente*.

3 Meanwhile, lightly beat the eggs in a bowl and add the Parmesan, a little salt, and a generous amount of black pepper.

4 Drain the pasta, reserving a cupful of the water. Return the spaghetti to the saucepan and toss with the butter, then add to the frying pan. Stir-fry a minute or so.

5 Remove from the heat and transfer the spaghetti mixture to a heated bowl. Pour over the egg and cheese mixture and add about 4 tablespoons of the reserved water to give the sauce the right fluidity. Mix well and serve at once.

Serves 3 as a main course or
4 as a first course

1 tablespoon olive oil
4 fresh sage leaves
1 garlic clove, peeled
$\frac{1}{4}$ pound smoked pancetta or bacon, cut into matchsticks
$\frac{3}{4}$ pound spaghetti
3 eggs
6 tablespoons freshly grated Parmesan cheese
salt and freshly ground black pepper
4 tablespoons butter

BAKED AND
STUFFED
PASTA

RAVIOLI DI PESCE

FISH RAVIOLI

Serves 4 as a main course

For the pasta dough
1⅓ cups flour
(preferably Italian 00)
2 extra large eggs
1 teaspoon olive oil
1 tablespoon oil
6 tablespoons unsalted butter
3 tablespoons very finely cut
fresh chives
freshly grated Parmesan
cheese, for serving

For the filling
4 tablespoons unsalted butter
2 tablespoons very finely
chopped onion
10 ounces skinless white fish
fillet, such as sole, flounder, sea
bass, or porgy
1 salted anchovy, boned and
rinsed, or 2 canned anchovy
fillets, drained
½ cup dry white wine
⅔ cup fresh ricotta cheese
¼ cup whipping cream
3 tablespoons freshly grated
Parmesan cheese
2 egg yolks
salt and freshly ground
black pepper

A new type of ravioli and a successful one. You can use any firm-fleshed fish including, of course, cod. The better the fish, the more tasty the ravioli!

1 First prepare the filling: Put the butter and onion in a saucepan and cook, stirring and pressing the onion against the side of the pan to release the flavor, about 5 minutes.

2 Meanwhile, cut the fish into very small pieces. Chop the anchovy. Add both to the onion and cook 1½–2 minutes.

3 Turn the heat up and splash in the wine, then boil rapidly until it has totally evaporated. Flake the fish coarsely. Transfer the mixture to a bowl and let cool a few minutes.

4 Add the ricotta to the fish mixture with the cream, Parmesan, and egg yolks. Season with salt and pepper and mix very well. Set aside while you make the pasta dough, following the instructions on page 9, adding the olive oil with the eggs.

5 Cut off one-quarter of the pasta dough, leaving the rest wrapped in plastic wrap. Thin the dough down in the pasta machine notch by notch as far as the last but one notch, as described on page 11. If you are rolling out by hand, roll the dough out as thin as you possibly can.

6 Work on one strip of dough at a time, keeping the remaining strips covered with a dish towel. Place mounds of the filling about ½ teaspoon each in a straight line along the length of the strip of dough spacing them about 1½ inches apart and the same distance from the one long edge. Fold the dough lengthwise over the filling and, using a pasta wheel, trim the edges where they meet. Then cut into squares between each mound of filling. Separate the squares and squeeze out any air that may be caught in the ravioli. Seal them tight with moistened fingers.

7 Place the ravioli on clean, dry dish towels, well separated. Cut off another quarter of the dough, knead in any trimmings from the previous batch, and thin the strip down as before. If you are rolling out by hand keep the dough you are not working on well covered or it will dry out and become brittle. Continue making more ravioli until you have used up all the filling and/or all the dough. Leave the ravioli uncovered until they are properly dry; you can then cover them with another cloth.

8 Bring a large saucepan of water to a boil. Add the oil and $1\frac{1}{2}$ tablespoons of salt. Drop the ravioli gently into the pan and bring the water back to a boil. Adjust the heat so that the water boils gently; if it boils too fast the ravioli might break. Cook until they are done, about 4–5 minutes, stirring gently every now and then. The best way to tell if they are done is to try one: The pasta should be still firm to the bite, *al dente*, at the edge. Lift the ravioli out with a slotted spoon and transfer them immediately to a heated and buttered bowl. Pat them dry with paper towels.

9 While the ravioli are cooking, melt the butter in a small saucepan. Stir in the chives. Pour this sauce over the ravioli. Serve at once, passing the grated Parmesan in a separate bowl.

LASAGNE AL FORNO

BAKED LASAGNE

Serves 4–6

homemade lasagne, made with
3 extra large eggs and 2¼ cups
flour (page 9) or 1½ pounds
bought fresh lasagne
Bolognese sauce
(page 32)
1 tablespoon salt
1 tablespoon vegetable or
olive oil
⅔ cup freshly grated
Parmesan cheese
1 tablespoon butter

For the béchamel sauce
3 cups whole milk
6 tablespoons unsalted butter
6 tablespoons flour flavored with
2 pinches of grated nutmeg

Few dishes have been so badly copied abroad as baked
lasagne, a dish that surely has acquired an appalling image.
Yet when well made, it is one of the finest creations of the very
rich Bolognese cuisine. While I might occasionally be pushed to
use store-bought fresh tagliatelle, I find store-bought lasagne
frankly not good enough.

This is a party dish, perfect for a family celebration. A certain
amount of time must be set aside to prepare it. So try to do
it properly and make your own pasta. The difference is quite
remarkable.

1 If you are making your own lasagne, lay the pasta rectangles out, separate from each other, on clean dish towels.

2 While the bolognese sauce is cooking, make the béchamel. You will find the recipe on page 48.

3 Choose a large sauté pan. Fill it with water and add the salt and oil. When the water is boiling, slide in five or six lasagne at a time. Move them around with a wooden fork to stop them sticking to each other. When they are *al dente*, lift them out with a slotted spatula and plunge them into a bowl of cold water. Lift out, lay on dish towels, and pat dry with paper towels.

4 Heat the oven to 425°F.

5 Butter a 12- × 8-inch ovenproof dish. Spread 2 tablespoons of the bolognese sauce on the bottom. Cover with a layer of lasagne and spread over 2 tablespoons or so of bolognese and the same of béchamel sauce. Sprinkle with a little Parmesan. Repeat, building up the dish in thin layers until you have used up all the ingredients. The top layer must be béchamel.

6 Dot with the butter and bake 20 minutes. Remove from the oven and leave at least 5 minutes before serving so the flavors can develop.

IL RAVIOLONE

PASTA AND SPINACH ROLL

Serves 6 as a main course,
8 as a first course

1½ pounds frozen leaf spinach,
thawed, or 3 pounds fresh bulk
spinach
salt and freshly ground
black pepper
3 tablespoons very finely
chopped shallots
2 tablespoons unsalted butter
1 cup fresh ricotta cheese
¾ cup freshly grated
Parmesan cheese
½ teaspoon grated nutmeg
1 egg yolk
homemade pasta dough, made
with 1⅓ cups flour, the yolks of
4 extra large eggs, and just
enough cold water to help the
dough absorb the flour (page 9)
4 large slices of unsmoked ham

For dressing the roll
6 tablespoons unsalted butter,
heated with 1 bruised garlic
clove and 4–6 fresh sage leaves,
or a thin béchamel sauce
(see Note opposite)
freshly grated Parmesan cheese

In this dish the procedure for stuffing pasta is different. The whole sheet of pasta dough is rolled around the spinach filling. The roll is sliced when cold, just like a boned roast, and then heated up in the oven with its sauce. It results in a very attractive presentation.

1 If you are using frozen spinach, cook the thawed spinach in a covered pan with a little salt, about 5 minutes. If you are using fresh spinach, discard any wilted or discolored spinach leaves and the tougher stems. Wash it, and then cook in a covered pan with just the water that clings to the leaves and with a little salt until tender, 5–8 minutes. Drain the spinach, squeezing lightly to remove most of its moisture. Set aside.

2 In a frying pan, sauté the chopped shallot in the butter over medium heat. When the shallot turns pale gold in color, add the spinach and sauté 5 minutes, turning the spinach over and over to *insaporire* – take up the flavor.

3 Transfer the contents of the frying pan to a food processor and add the ricotta, grated Parmesan, nutmeg, and, last of all, the egg yolk. Process a few seconds. Check the seasoning.

4 Roll out the pasta dough into as thin a sheet as possible, about 15 × 20 inches. Lay it flat in front of you. Square the sides to make a neat rectangle.

5 Place the ham slices to cover the pasta rectangle completely, leaving a clean edge of about 1 inch on all sides.

6 Spread the spinach filling over the ham. Roll up as for a jelly roll by first making a pleat and then rolling fairly tightly. Wrap the pasta roll tightly in cheesecloth and tie the two ends securely with string.

7 Use a fish kettle or other long, deep pan that can hold the roll comfortably and about 4 quarts of water. Bring the water to a boil, add about 2 tablespoons of salt, and then put in the pasta roll. Cook at a gentle but steady boil, about 35 minutes.

8 Lift out the roll. Unwrap it while it is hot and set it aside to cool, loosely covered with foil.

9 Heat the oven to 400°F.

10 Cut the roll into $\frac{1}{2}$-inch slices with a very sharp knife or an electric knife. (It is easier to slice the *rotolo* when cool.)

11 Place the slices in a generously buttered shallow baking dish, overlapping them a little. You can dress the slices with either the garlic- and sage-flavored butter and then a generous amount of Parmesan, or with a layer of Parmesan covered with the thin, well-flavored béchamel. Cover the dish with foil and bake 15–20 minutes. Remove from the oven and leave 5 minutes before serving.

Note: For a thin béchamel, use 3 cups whole milk, 5 tablespoons unsalted butter, and 3 tablespoons flour. Follow the recipe on page 48, heating the milk with 1 bay leaf.

PASTA 'NCACIATA

EGGPLANT AND RIGATONI CAKE

Serves 6 as a first course or
4–5 as a main course

2 eggplants, total weight about
1 pound
salt and freshly ground
black pepper
vegetable oil for frying
1 pound penne or rigatoni
4 tablespoons butter
double quantity plain tomato
sauce (page 19, bottom)
$\frac{1}{2}$ pound Italian mozzarella
cheese, coarsely grated or
chopped
$\frac{1}{4}$ cup freshly grated
Parmesan cheese
$\frac{1}{4}$ cup freshly grated aged
romano cheese
1 tablespoon dried oregano
2 tablespoons dry white
bread crumbs

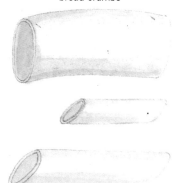

This is a very showy southern Italian dish traditionally baked in a dome-shaped container, which can be tricky to unmold. In this recipe I suggest using a springform cake pan. It can be prepared a few hours in advance.

1 Cut the eggplants into $\frac{1}{4}$-inch slices. Place a board on the slant over the sink. Put layers of eggplant slices on the board, sprinkling each layer with salt. Let drain 1 hour. Rinse thoroughly and pat each slice dry.

2 Heat enough oil in a large frying pan to come about 1 inch up the sides of the pan. The oil is hot enough when a corner of an eggplant slice dipped into it sizzles. Slide in a few slices of eggplant at a time and fry until deep golden on both sides. Do not overcrowd the slices or they will not fry properly.

3 Remove the fried eggplants with a slotted spoon, drain well, and place in a dish lined with paper towels.

4 Cook the rigatoni in plenty of boiling salted water until very *al dente*. Drain and return the rigatoni to the saucepan in which they were cooked. Toss with the butter. Mix in the tomato sauce, the three cheeses, oregano, and pepper to taste. Check the seasoning.

5 Heat the oven to 375°F.

6 Line the bottom of an 8-inch springform cake pan with eggplant slices. Fill in any gaps with cut-up pieces of eggplant. Line the sides of the pan with eggplant slices, cutting to fit. Place any eggplant left over on the bottom of the pan. Fill the pan with the rigatoni mixture and press down lightly. Sprinkle with the bread crumbs.

7 Bake until the filling is hot, about 20 minutes.

8 Remove from the oven and run a metal spatula around the side of the pan. Place a heated round serving dish over the top of the pan and turn the pan upside down. Tap the base of the pan and give the dish a sharp shake or two. Unclip the ring and lift the pan away carefully. If necessary, press into place any pieces of eggplant stuck to the pan. Let the cake stand at least 5 minutes for the flavors to combine.

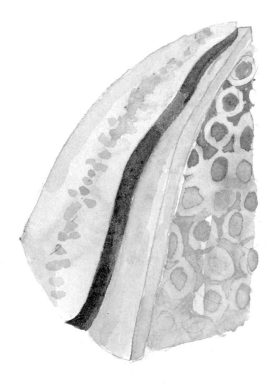

PASTA AL GRATIN
MACARONI AND CHEESE

Serves 4 as a first course or
3 as a main course

$\frac{1}{2}$ cup grated fontina cheese
$\frac{1}{2}$ cup freshly grated Parmesan
cheese
$\frac{3}{4}$ pound penne or maccheroni

For the béchamel sauce
3 cups whole milk
6 tablespoons unsalted butter
6 tablespoons flour
salt and freshly ground
black pepper
grated nutmeg

Years ago, at the beginning of my married life in England, my husband asked me which was my favorite pasta dish. "Very difficult question," I answered. Recently, however, when he asked me the same question, I said "Pasta al gratin". "Oh really?" he said, and thought "What about that discerning palate she's so proud of?" But he was thinking of the macaroni and cheese of his school days, and I was thinking of the velvety, cheesey delight of Pasta al Gratin.

Although it is made with a sauce with a French name, the dish is Italian. It is made in many regions, with certain variations. In the North, for instance, Parmesan is used, sometimes mixed with emmental or with fontina, as in my recipe, while in Naples a buffalo mozzarella is cut up and pushed here and there among the penne.

For all its simplicity, Pasta al Gratin needs a careful and patient cook, able to make a velvety béchamel and to drain the pasta at the right time, i.e. when still slightly undercooked, so that it can reach the right texture during baking.

1 To make the béchamel sauce, heat the milk until hot but not boiling. Remove from the heat.
2 Melt the butter in a saucepan, remove from the heat, and stir in the flour. Put the pan back on the heat and cook, stirring constantly, about half a minute.
3 Remove the pan from the heat again and add the milk gradually. At the beginning add only a couple of tablespoons and incorporate well, before adding another few tablespoons. Adding the milk slowly in this way helps prevent the flour forming lumps. Return the pan to the heat and cook until the sauce comes to a boil.

Season with salt and pepper and with a generous grating of nutmeg. Cook a few minutes, stirring constantly.

4 To finish the sauce you can either use a flame-tamer under the pan, or you can put the pan into a larger saucepan of simmering water – the water bath method. Let the sauce cook very, very gently about 30 minutes; you only need to stir occasionally. This long, slow cooking makes a rich, velvety sauce that you would not be able to achieve if you only cooked the béchamel 5 minutes, that is, just enough to cook the flour.

5 Add the cheeses to the béchamel. Taste and adjust the seasoning.

6 Cook the pasta in plenty of boiling salted water until very *al dente*. Drain thoroughly (penne tend to hold water in their hollows).

7 Heat the oven to 350°F.

8 Coat a shallow baking dish (about 2 inches deep) with a little of the sauce. Dress the pasta with about two-thirds of the béchamel and transfer to the prepared dish. Spread the rest of the sauce all over the top. Bake until the penne at the top begin to brown, about 30 minutes.

9 Leave out of the oven for 5 minutes before serving, to allow the flavors to blend while cooling a little.

GRAN MUGNAIO

Spadoni

ACETO

METODO LENTO A TRUCIOLO

Leonardo Spadoni

0,50 ℓe   7.45%

OTHER
FAVORITES

TAGLIATELLE AL BURRO E FORMAGGIO
——— TAGLIATELLE WITH BUTTER AND PARMESAN ———

Serves 4 as a first course or
3 as a main course

homemade tagliatelle, made
with 2 extra large eggs and $1\frac{1}{3}$
cups flour (page 9)
salt
$\frac{1}{2}$ cup freshly grated
Parmesan cheese
4 tablespoons best-quality
unsalted butter

In my home in Milan, when I was a child, special butter was used for this sauce. The best farm butter was sold, cut in pieces and wrapped in cheesecloth, by the best grocer in Via Monte Napoleone. And the tagliatelle were, of course, homemade.

This recipe is characteristic of northern Italian cooking. It is also the dressing used when you are lucky enough to have a white truffle to shave over it. To do the dish justice, you should make your own pasta and buy the best unsalted butter, as well as making sure your Parmesan is a proper Parmigiano Reggiano, of which you grate an ample quantity just before serving.

1 Cook the pasta in plenty of boiling salted water until *al dente*. Drain – but do not overdrain – and turn half the pasta into a heated serving bowl. Add about half of the cheese and stir well.
2 Cut the butter into small pieces and add half to the bowl. Toss thoroughly, then add the remaining cheese. Add the remaining butter and toss until all the butter has melted. Serve at once.

In Milan, more cheese is passed separately in a bowl.

TAGLIOLINI PICCANTI FREDDI

TAGLIOLINI WITH A PIQUANT SUN-DRIED TOMATO SAUCE

I do not usually like cold pasta, but I make a few exceptions. This is the best cold pasta dish I know, and it has always been a great success at my demonstrations.

When I have no time to make my tagliolini, I prefer to use a good brand of dried tagliolini such as Cipriani or Spinosi, rather than store-bought fresh pasta.

For this recipe buy loose sun-dried tomatoes that you reconstitute, not the kind under oil.

---

1 To reconstitute the sun-dried tomatoes, put them in a bowl. Heat $\frac{7}{8}$ cup of water with the wine vinegar, and when just boiling pour over the tomatoes. Let soak at least 2 hours.

2 Lift the tomatoes out of the liquid, lay them on a wooden board, and dry each one thoroughly with kitchen paper towels. Cut them into thin strips and put in a bowl large enough to hold the pasta later. Add the oil, chili peppers, garlic, and basil.

3 Cook the tagliolini in plenty of boiling salted water. Drain it when it is even more *al dente* than you would like for eating it hot. (Overcooked cold pasta is really unpleasant.) Turn the pasta into the bowl and toss very thoroughly, lifting the strands up high so as to separate them. Let infuse 2 hours or so, then remove the garlic and discard. Scatter the olives on top and serve.

Serves 4 as a first course

6 ounces sun-dried tomatoes
$\frac{1}{2}$ cup wine vinegar
6 tablespoons extra virgin olive oil
1 or 2 small dried chili peppers, according to taste, strength, and size, seeded and crumbled
5 garlic cloves, bruised
a dozen fresh basil leaves, torn into small pieces
11 ounces dried tagliolini, or homemade tagliolini made with 2 extra large eggs and $1\frac{1}{3}$ cups flour (page 9)
salt
$\frac{1}{2}$ cup black olives, such as Kalamata

TAGLIARDI E ZUCCHINE AL SUGO DI PISTACCHIO E BASILICO

TAGLIARDI AND ZUCCHINI WITH A
PISTACHIO NUT AND BASIL SAUCE

Serves 6 as a first course or
4 as a main course

homemade green pasta dough,
made with 3 extra large eggs,
2½ cups flour
and 1¼ cups cooked spinach
(page 9), or ½ pound bought
green tagliatelle or tagliardi
⅞ cup extra virgin olive oil,
preferably from Sicily or Puglia
4 garlic cloves, bruised
1¼ pounds zucchini, cut
into matchsticks
salt and freshly ground
black pepper
½ cup shelled pistachio nuts
1 cup fresh basil
⅔ cup fresh flat-leaf Italian parsley
1 tablespoon unsalted butter

Last year, during a short visit to Sicily, I had more interesting pasta dishes than during many a year in London. The pistachio and basil sauce was prepared for a dinner in the garden by Vittoria Spadaro, a friend and a good cook who is passionate about the great tradition of her island's cooking. The combination of flavors and the presentation of this dish epitomize the very best of Sicilian cooking.

The pasta used by Vittoria was green pappardelle which she made herself. If you do not have the time or inclination to make your own pasta I suggest you buy a box of the excellent tagliardi made by Cipriani, available in good Italian grocers. It is the best egg pasta on the market. It has a delicate silky texture that is normally found only in homemade pasta. Cipriani pasta is expensive, but when cooked it grows in volume more than any other pasta. And it is so good that it is well worth its higher price.

1 If you are making your own pasta, roll it and cut into pappardelle (page 12). Spread the pasta out on clean dish towels while you make the sauce.

2 Heat 2 tablespoons of the oil and the garlic in a nonstick frying pan. When hot, add the zucchini and fry at a lively heat until golden all over. Shake the pan very often. They are ready whey they are tender, not still crunchy but not yet soft, and when the flavor has fully developed – about 15 minutes. Season with salt and pepper.

3 While the zucchini are frying, put the pistachios into a small saucepan. Cover with water, bring to a boil, and boil 10 seconds.

Skin the pistachios, taking them out of the hot water a few at a time for easier peeling. Dry them thoroughly and put in a food processor.

4 Rinse and dry the basil and parsley and add to the pistachios. Process while adding the rest of the oil through the hole in the lid. Stop the machine, push the mixture down from the side of the bowl, and process again a few seconds. Add salt and pepper to taste. Scoop out the mixture into a serving bowl and place the bowl in a warm oven.

5 Cook the pasta in plenty of salted boiling water until *al dente*. Drain, reserving a cupful of the pasta water, and turn immediately into the heated bowl. Add the butter and toss very thoroughly, adding 3 or 4 tablespoons of the reserved water to give the pasta the right fluidity.

6 Spoon the zucchini and their juices over the top of the pasta and serve at once.

CONCHIGLIE DI RADICCHIO ROSSO COL RIPIENO DI PASTA

RED RADICCHIO LEAVES FILLED WITH PASTA

Serves 4 as a first course

a bunch of fresh flat-leaf
Italian parsley
1 garlic clove
2 salted anchovies, boned and
rinsed or 4 canned anchovy
fillets, drained
1 small dried chili pepper
$\frac{1}{4}$ cup extra virgin olive oil
salt
$\frac{1}{2}$ pound ditali or gnocchi
4 outside leaves from a large
head of red radicchio
freshly ground black pepper
(optional)

Although I am not very keen on pasta salads, I am not as hostile toward them as one woman evidently was, judging by a recent report in *The Times* of London.

"Laurette Bruson threw macaroni salad at Richard, her groom, during a tiff at their wedding reception in Tampa, Florida, and he responded by shooting her with a .22 pistol."

This salad is an attractive dish, definitely not for throwing, with the shiny ditali tasting mainly of olive oil. I use a peppery oil for this dish, such as an extra virgin oil from Chianti or a fruity and herby oil from Sicily or Puglia.

If you cannot find a large radicchio head, use a Bibb or Boston lettuce.

1 Chop the parsley, garlic, and anchovies and put them in a large bowl with the whole chili pepper. Beat in the oil and add salt to taste.

2 Cook the pasta in plenty of boiling salted water, remembering that cold pasta needs to be more *al dente* than hot pasta. Drain, refresh under cold water, and drain again thoroughly. Pat dry with paper towels. Turn the pasta into the bowl with the dressing and toss well. Let infuse about 2 hours.

3 Wash and dry the radicchio leaves thoroughly and lay them on individual plates.

4 Remove the chili from the dressing and discard it. Taste and add pepper, if liked. Fill the salad leaves with the pasta just before serving.

LIST OF RECIPES